# The Dog

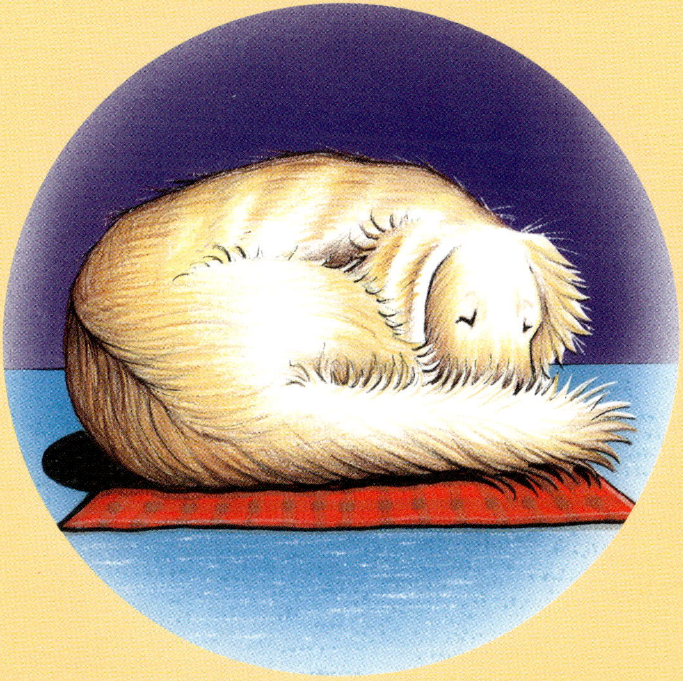

Story by Gloria Bancroft

Illustrations by Peter Townsend

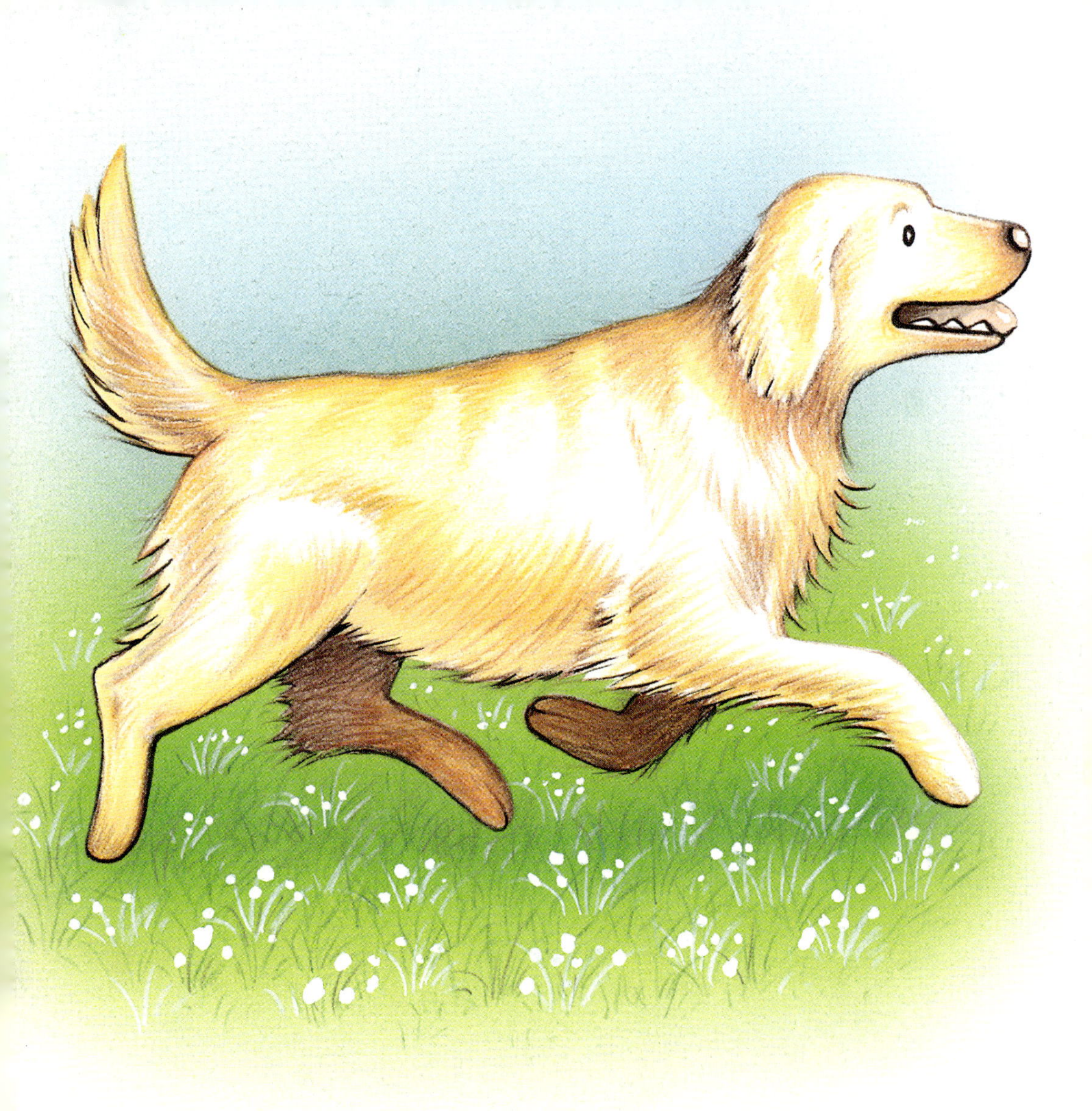

The dog can run.

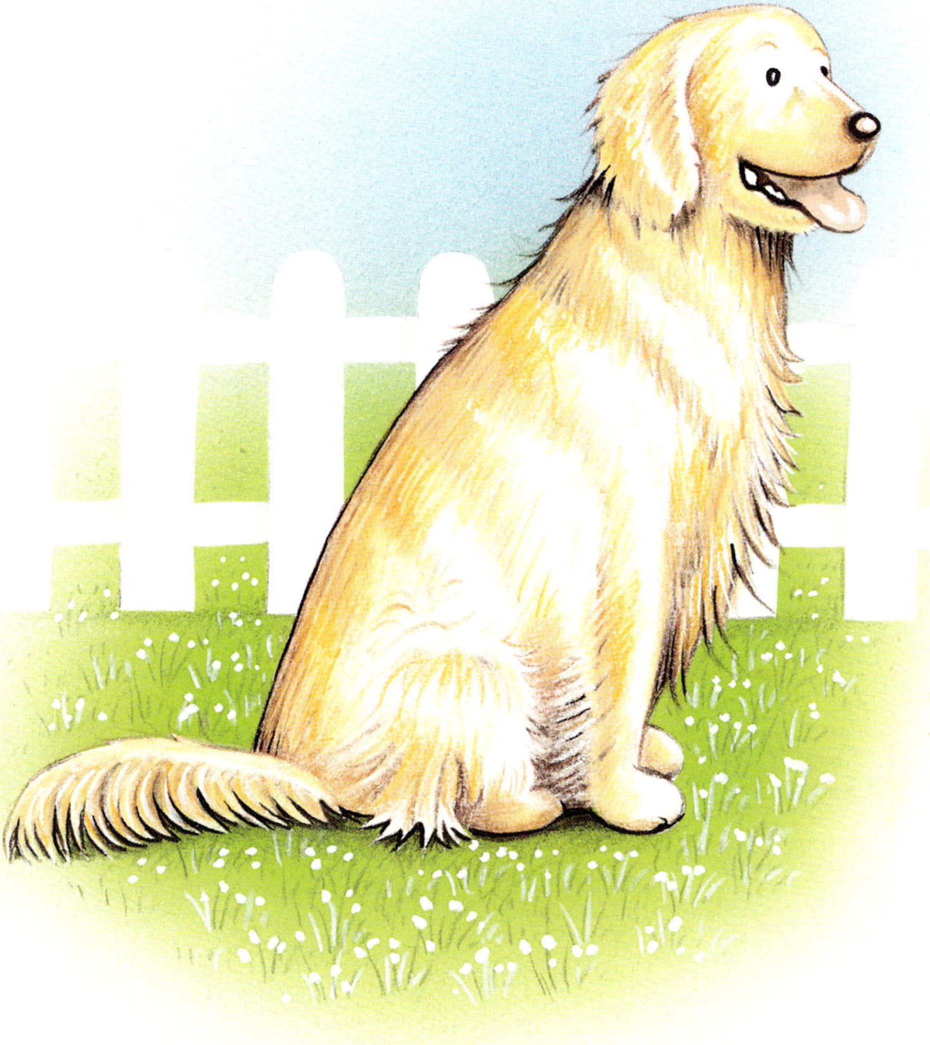

The dog can sit.

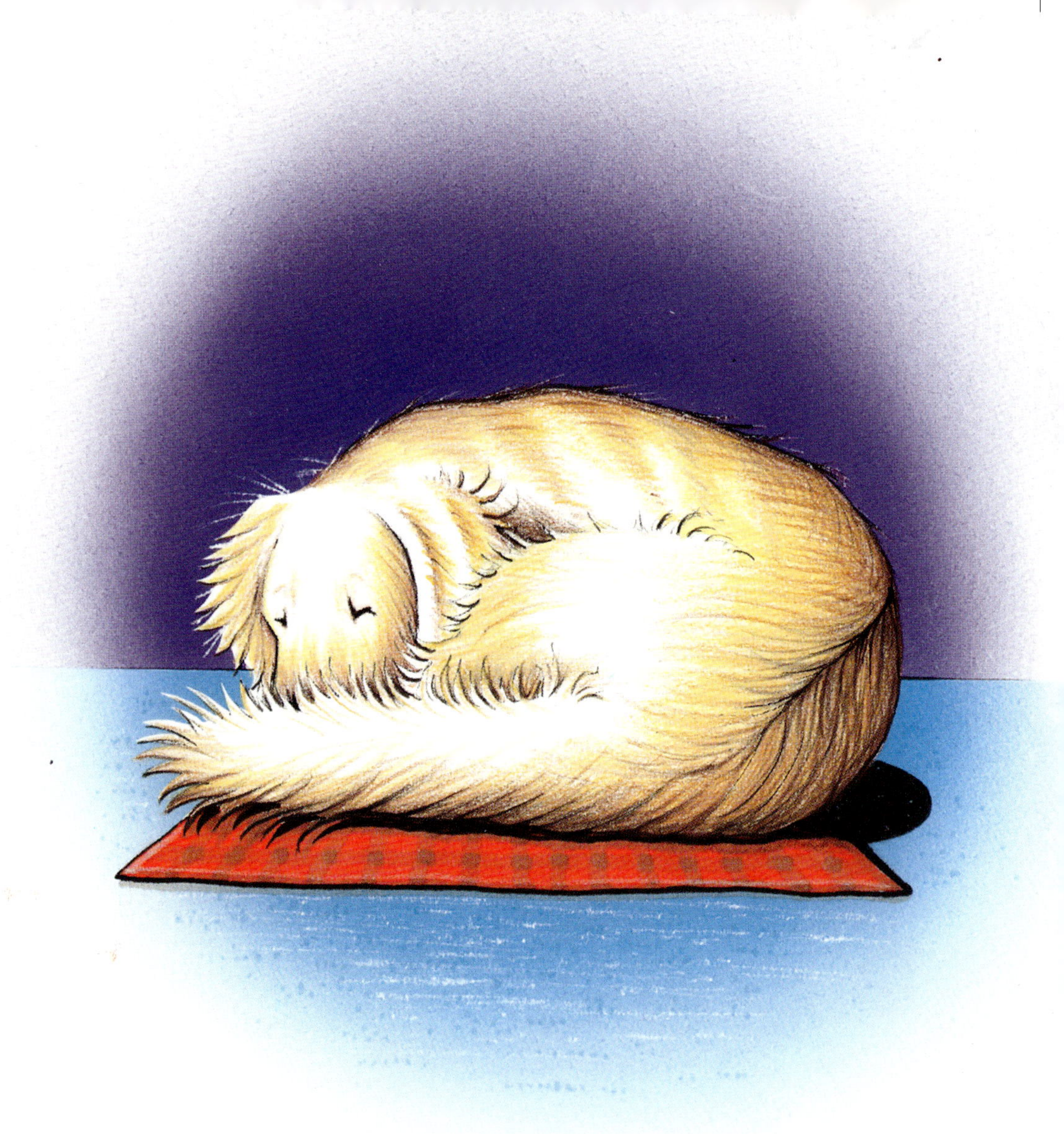

The dog can sleep.

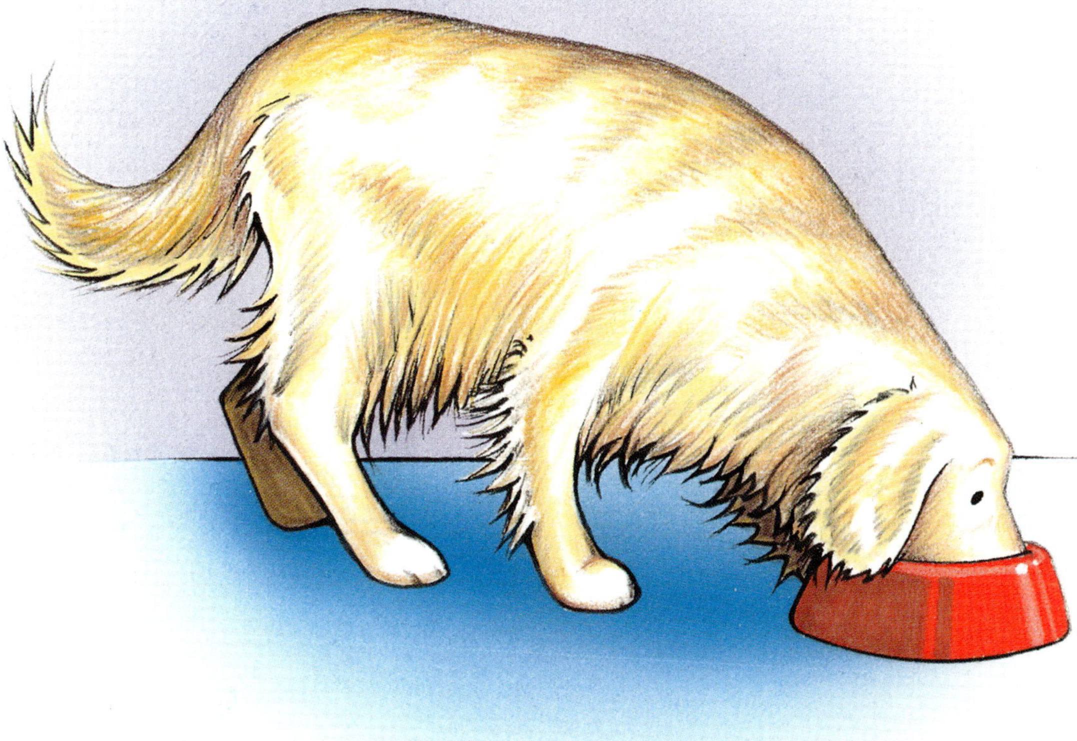

The dog can eat.

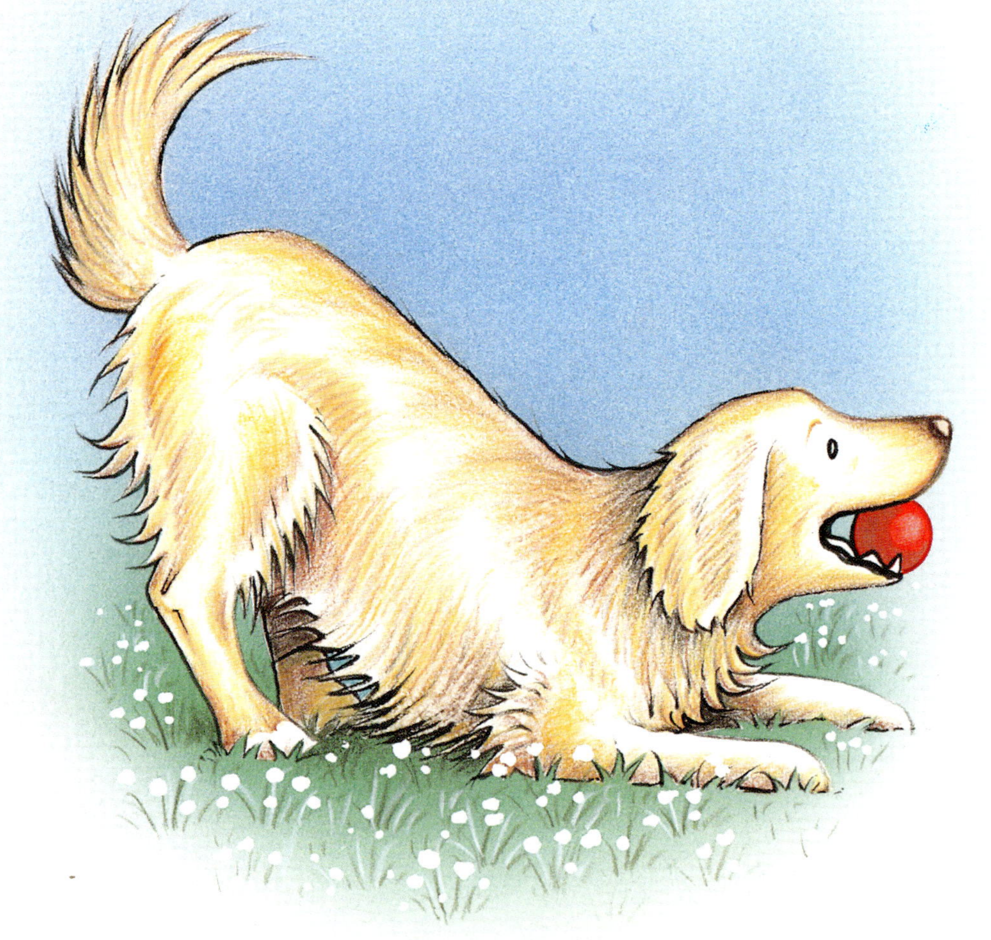

The dog can play.

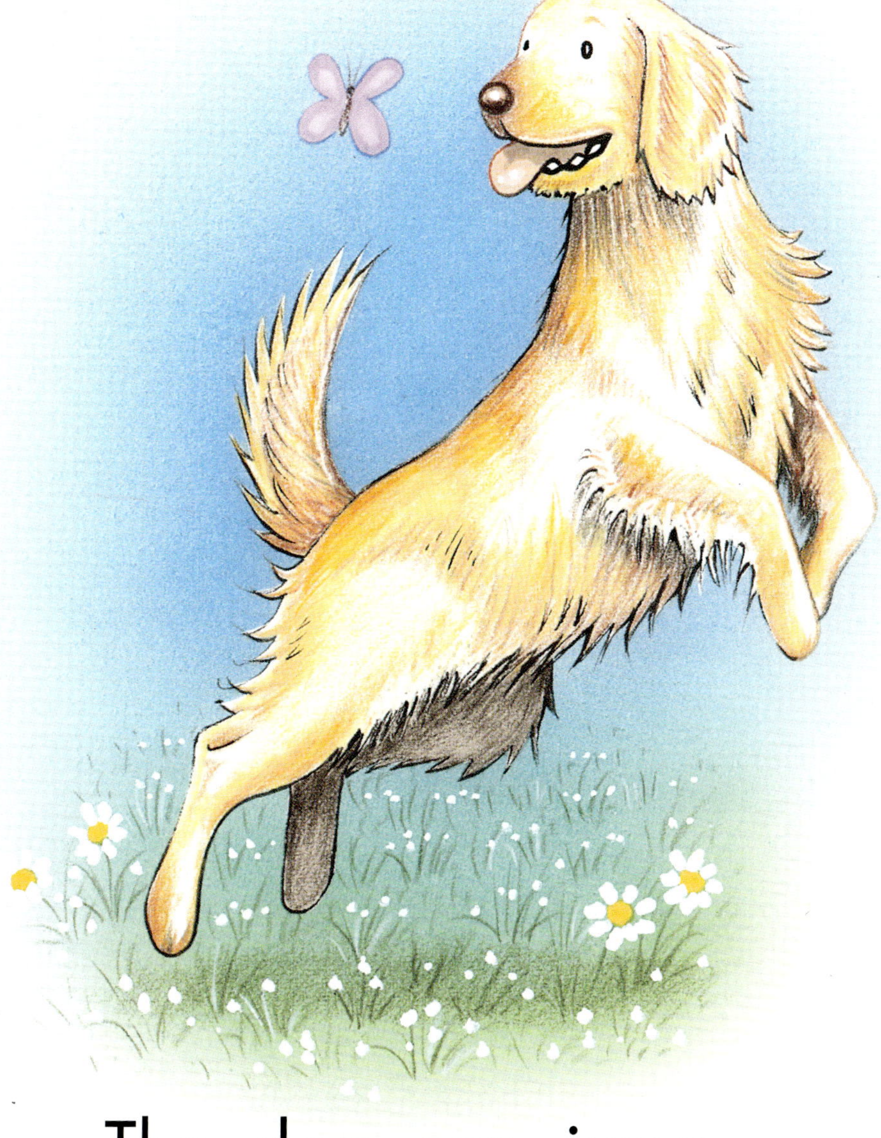

The dog can jump.

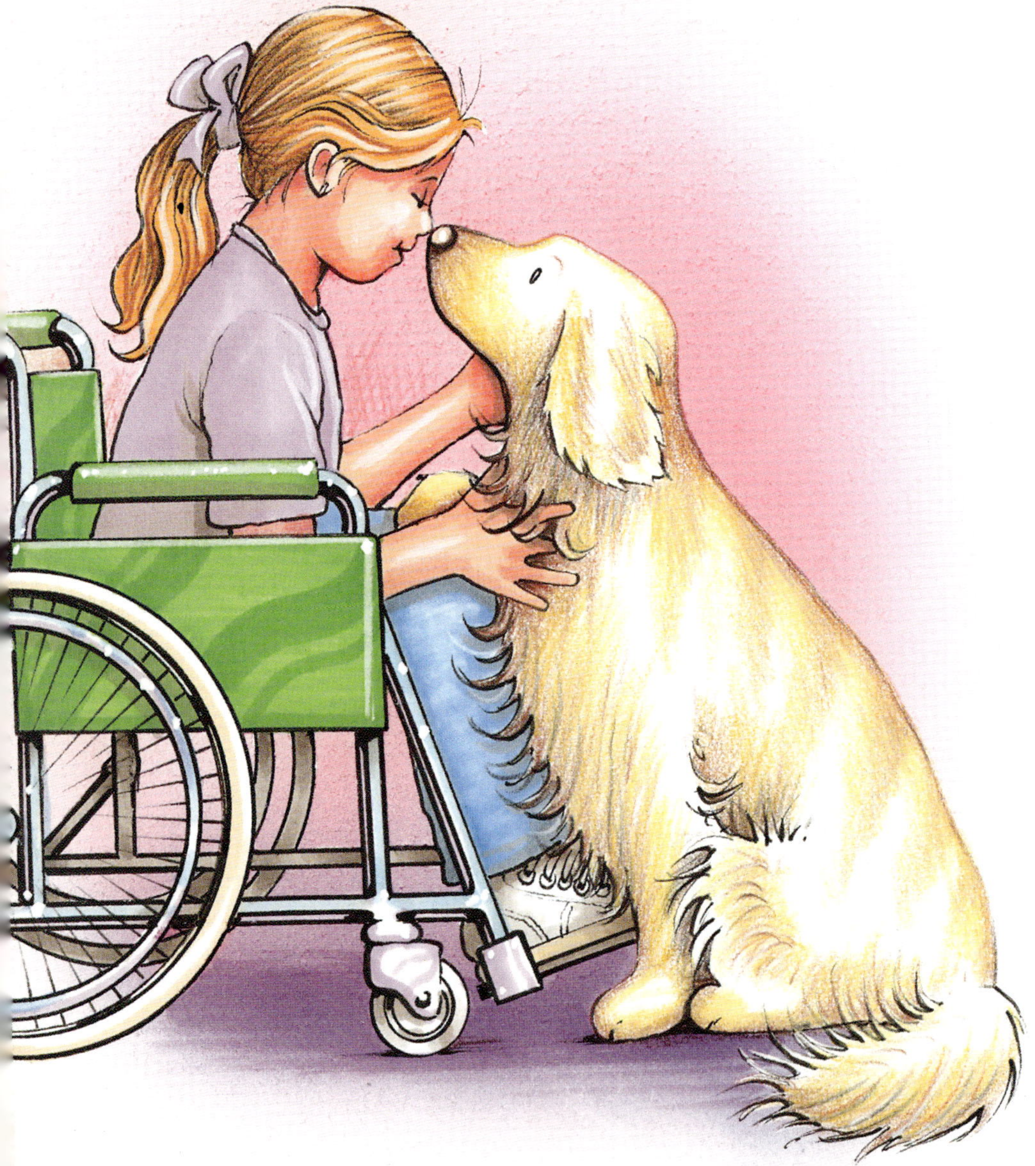

The dog can kiss.